TOO MANY PEOPLE?

CHRISTOPHER DERRICK

Too Many People?

A Problem in Values

IGNATIUS PRESS   SAN FRANCISCO

Cover by Victoria Hoke
With ecclesiastical approval
©1985 Ignatius Press, San Francisco
ISBN 0-89870-071-X
Library of Congress Catalogue Number 85-060469
Printed in the United States of America

Contents

72325

I

Problem and Solution?

This book is written for a highly specific purpose. I hope to broaden the scope of Christian attention—of Catholic attention in particular—to the much-debated question of population control. Too many of us are concerned only with the morality of the means: I suggest that we should also pay attention to the implied value judgments, the entire mental 'set' that causes so many of us to see population as a 'problem', to which we must find a 'solution' if we can. To a degree that can easily be overlooked, these differ from the value judgments and the mental 'set' of Christian faith and tradition.

If I propose to consider them from the standpoint of an unreconstructed Roman Catholic, strictly orthodox or traditional in the Faith, let no reader take fright. This is not another book about the disputed questions of sexual morality, and I have in fact practically nothing to say here about the rights and wrongs of contraception and abortion and sterilisation—not because I dissent from Catholic tradition in such matters, but

because they don't form part of my present subject. My case depends in no way upon the Pope,
but only upon what C. S. Lewis called 'mere
Christianity'.

The question of world population, and of its
possible control, has come in for a great deal of
public discussion in recent decades and has been
the subject of two major United Nations Conferences, at Bucharest in 1974 and at Mexico City in
1984: I attended the former but not the latter. The
subject has aroused a great deal of public concern,
even of public alarm. But such feelings appear to
have varied considerably in intensity. They seem
to have reached a kind of peak in the early 1970s,
but to have subsided after the Bucharest Conference: other anxieties appear to have taken their
place in the headlines and in the public attention.
Early in 1984, as the Mexico City Conference
drew near, various public figures found it necessary to underline its importance, to insist that
over-population was still one of the most serious
dangers confronting mankind. But the world took
little notice. In the English press at least, that second Conference received only the most per-
functory sort of coverage.

This book may therefore appear some ten or
fifteen years too late, its subject being no longer
'hot': the reader will note that most of the works

cited date from the 1960s and 1970s. I make only the faintest apology for such tardiness. The subject is most unlikely to remain cold for ever; it will hit the headlines once again before too long, and in any case, the philosophical aspect of the subject—as distinct from its statistical and political and journalistic aspects—is of perennial importance.

To some extent, I here offer an analysis of how certain people were talking, and indeed shouting, some twelve years ago. But I do not write in the past tense. In so far as it succeeds, this book is also an analysis of how millions are undoubtedly still thinking, and may soon be talking and shouting once again.

Concern about population is no kind of novelty, nor is the idea of subjecting it to public control. In the *Republic* and even more strongly in the *Laws*, Plato called for a static population, and so for the alternate prohibition and encouragement of large families, as appropriate. Developing this theme, Aristotle said that superfluous children should not be killed directly: they should be exposed or abandoned, the responsibility for their fate being thereby thrown upon the gods.

Many similar policies and practices are reported by the historians and the anthropologists. It is as well to remember that the problem has not always been seen in terms of 'too many people', as *The Vicar of Wakefield* reminds us in its very first sentence: "I was ever of opinion, that the honest man who married and brought up a large family, did more service than he who continued single and only talked of population". Goldsmith's novel appeared only thirty-two years before the celebrated *Essay on the Principle of Population* by Thomas Malthus.

Under-population has frequently been feared, for economic and military reasons among others. Well into this century, even in the 1930s, the growing practice of contraception was widely denounced—in France and elsewhere—as making for 'national suicide', this being chiefly seen in terms of 'not enough soldiers'. Even today, it is generally acknowledged that in a rich country, a falling birth-rate causes a larger geriatric population to become dependent upon a smaller working population, so generating much economic and social stress.

But when 'the population problem' comes up for present-day discussion, it is almost invariably seen in terms of 'too many people', existing now or in the more or less immediate future.

As so understood, the problem finds its most general and abstract expression in the undeniable truth that there cannot be infinite growth within a closed system; and for all practical purposes, this planet *is* a closed system. Plans for the large-scale colonisation of outer space belong strictly within the realm of science fiction.

From that basic truth, we can move on—still at a high level of abstraction—to the famous 'principle' of Malthus. But we must do so cautiously. Malthus was a mathematician, and he knew the difference between simple and compound interest, between growth-rates that are arithmetical and those that are geometric or exponential. He was therefore right in saying that on paper, population is capable of increasing exponentially and (unless checked by human or natural factors) 'infinitely', with no theoretical upper limit.

He made two mistakes. He did less than justice to the complex psychological and motivational factors that govern our reproductive behaviour in fact; and when he said that our production of food and other necessities could only increase arithmetically, he was guilty of an arbitrary guess. But on the information available to him, it was not a foolish guess. He had no means of knowing that technological development would soon increase every sort of productivity in the most spectacular way.

Conversely, two mistakes are made *about* Malthus. It is often suggested, as by Aldous

Huxley in *Brave New World,* that he favoured contraception: in fact, he looked upon that practice with the moral revulsion that was common to all Christians (and to many others) until very recently. Then, it is often suggested that he was proposing some kind of 'solution' to some kind of 'population problem': in fact, he was chiefly concerned to refute the revolutionary Utopianism of Godwin and Condorcet. Not all problems are soluble, he insisted: the condition of the poor must always be wretched, incapable of improvement, and anything like the Welfare State—which then existed in an extremely rudimentary form—can only make their condition worse. The English class system involved certain extremes of what would now be called 'social injustice'. Nonetheless, Malthus stoutly maintained that, while one can always dream, nothing better was capable of being achieved in actual fact.

He was what we would now call a man of the fairly extreme Right, furiously denounced as such by Proudhon the anarchist, also by Karl Marx and his followers and the Left generally—a pattern which has continued to haunt all discussions of population and poverty.[1]

The condition of the English poor *has* been im-

---

[1] See Appendix.

proved since his day, and most dramatically: Malthus was quite wrong about that. But as regards the pure mathematics of human reproduction, he was broadly and unquestionably correct.

So, as we approach the bicentenary of his *Essay*, we see the outcome of that mathematical principle. Human numbers are now larger than ever before, and are *therefore* increasing more rapidly than ever before. That's the broad picture, varying from time to time and from place to place but globally predominant. We are all familiar with those graphs of world population, rising slowly over the centuries and millennia and then exploding upwards in more recent times.

What will be the future pattern of that curve? In the closed system of this world, it certainly cannot continue ever-more-steeply upwards for ever. Many writers have played mathematical games with the idea of it doing exactly that: they soon reach the picture of a standing-room-only world, and they sometimes go beyond it into realms of even higher absurdity.

But no informed person supposes that anything remotely like that is going to happen in fact. The usual and most plausible prediction is that if world population continues to increase at its present exponential rate, perfectly 'natural' factors (such as

the Four Horsemen of the Apocalypse) will inter-
vene, causing it to level off at some point and
perhaps to decline sharply. That often happens to
animal populations in the wild: will it happen to
Homo sapiens as well?

That depends upon how *sapiens* he shows himself to be. We face a choice. The human population
will certainly level off some day and may then
decline. But is this to happen in Nature's way,
which is highly efficient but involves great hardship? or can we cause it to happen in some more
controlled and human fashion, involving very
much less hardship?

That's how the 'problem' is usually stated, on
the rather precarious assumption that the choice is
a real one and that an unspecified 'we' are capable
of making it effectively; and it's interesting to note
that the language used in this connection has a
marked tendency to be apocalyptic or eschatological. Nobody can look with pleasure upon any
great extension of hardship, of human suffering.
But it wouldn't be the end of the world; and many
people talk and write as though it would be exactly
and literally that—as though over-population
threatened not only our welfare and comfort but
our actual survival as a species.

By way of illustration, I shall cite a few instances
of this curious tendency: it pervades nearly all the

popular literature on the subject, and even some of the more specialised and scientific works, raising some interesting questions of motivation. Somebody should write a book called *The Psychology of Doomtalk*, about writers and about readers as well.

Paul Ehrlich is not, perhaps, the most reliable of authorities, and his best-selling book *The Population Bomb*,[2] which has been before the world for a long time now, offers much quiet amusement to those who enjoy seeing confident prophecy getting its comeuppance from subsequent fact. Nonetheless, I shall quote it from time to time in these pages, not for any reliability in matters of actual or probable fact, but only for its evidential value in respect of public opinion. Generally speaking, a book which sells in such numbers is a book which tells a great many people what they want to hear. It echoes sentiments which already prevail, and it also gives them powerful reinforcement.

We all know what 'the Bomb' means for the present-day consciousness, and Ehrlich was being apocalyptic in his very title. He developed that

[2] Paul Ehrlich, *The Population Bomb* (London and New York: Pan/Ballantine, 1972). Here and subsequently, the details given are those of the edition actually cited, and they are given once and for all. Other editions may differ in date and pagination and sometimes in text.

association of ideas at many points, constantly using the language of *finality*. "The birth rate must be brought into balance with the death rate or mankind will breed itself into *oblivion*."[3] It is hard to see exactly what is meant by "oblivion", but some sort of finality is clearly implied: it becomes explicit at other points. "Regardless of changes in technology or resource consumption and distribution, current rates of population growth guarantee an environmental crisis which will persist until *the final collapse*."[4]

The rhetoric of an excited writer should not always be taken literally. But very similar language is found in the writings of those who handle this subject in a very much more sober and scientific manner. "The transition from unlimited growth to rapid decline will not be pleasant. If it happens it will be within the lifetime of our children or grandchildren. There will be frequent crises, increasing disasters, and finally *collapse*."[5] That may be an unconscious echo of Ehrlich: neither author is clear about what sort of "collapse" he has in mind or how "finally" he expects it to happen. But the eschatological note is sounded clearly enough, becoming explicit later

[3] *The Population Bomb,* Prologue, emphasis added.

[4] *The Population Bomb,* 47, emphasis added.

[5] Derek Llewellyn-Jones, *People Populating* (London: Faber and Faber, 1975), 20-21, emphasis added.

on. "If the reader accepts that the exponential rate of population growth poses a major threat to the quality of life, that it aggravates the malnutrition in the hungry Third World, and that it is a threat to our very *survival* . . ."[6]: how are we to take those words? The word "our" might conceivably be intended as a disjunction from "the hungry Third World": the thing endangered would then be the "survival"—or perhaps the hegemony—of the white-skinned affluent West. But the concluding sentences of this book lie open to no such racialist interpretation. "Not only in China, but in all the nations of this very small planet, mankind's survival depends upon a rational approach to population control. But with good sense, and a bit of luck, we who live on this small planet will survive. If we act now. The choice lies in our hands."[7]

What can this author have supposed himself to mean? In what sense will "we" survive? As individuals, we shall all die: as a species, there are astronomical reasons (among others) for saying that we cannot continue for ever, while a Christian will have his own things to say about eschatology. But as a species—biologically considered—how is our "survival" endangered by over-population or by any of its possible consequences?

Instances of such over-dramatic terminology

[6] *People Populating*, 227, emphasis added.
[7] *People Populating*, 355.

could be multiplied indefinitely. *Limits to Growth*[8] is a book that made a great impression when it first appeared, chiefly because of the seeming rigour of its computerised method, which has been largely discredited by later work. But I am not concerned at the moment with statistical fact but only with manners of thinking; and it is noteworthy that those authors, after proposing their vast and implausible plan for saving us all, saw fit to say: "Only the conviction that there is no other avenue to *survival* can liberate the moral, intellectual, and creative forces required to initiate this unprecedented human undertaking."[9] In extenuation, it should be remembered that they were considering not only population but other environmental factors as well.

Countless writers, considering population alone, use language that would be more appropriate to an all-out nuclear holocaust. "We know that to stabilize the world's population is at some point a condition of *survival*":[10] those words come from no rhetorical journalist but from two au-

[8] Donella H. Meadows and others, *Limits to Growth (The Report for the Club of Rome)* (New York: Universe Books, 1972).

[9] *Limits to Growth,* 196, emphasis added.

[10] Barbara Ward and René Dubos, *Only One Earth* (London: Penguin Books, 1972), 176, emphasis added.

thorities of the highest reputation. In the same vein and more recently, a most influential High Priest of population-control was quoted as saying "the sooner population stabilises, the better", because "we want the species to *survive* on this planet."[11]

Any sort of case is weakened, not strengthened, by proponents who habitually argue it in the language of manifestly wild exaggeration.

For the sake of appeal and impact, doomtalk always needs to exaggerate. If you say, "Something distinctly unpleasant is rather likely to happen", nobody will take much interest. But if you say, "Something utterly and finally disastrous is quite certain to happen!", people will love you for it. Your book will sell.

But you always need to add an "unless . . . ." Nobody wants unqualified despair.

So this final and absolute doom is certain to come upon us all, *unless* we succeed in lowering birth-rates substantially, universally, and on a permanent basis.

But how are 'we' to do that? Malthus recommended late marriage and sexual restraint—to the

---

[11] Dr. Rafael M. Salas, Director of the United Nations Fund for Population Activities, just before the Mexico City Conference of 1984: *Newsweek* (European edition), August 13, 1984, emphasis added once again.

poor, that is—and if we all took that advice, birth-rates would undoubtedly fall. But we seem rather unlikely to take it.

That leaves us with either or both of two options. We can try to alleviate poverty wherever it co-exists with over-population, and we can then hope that the 'demographic transition' will lower birth-rates more or less automatically. Most of us would say that poverty should be alleviated in any case. But the practical difficulties are enormous; and even if these were to be overcome, nobody understands the 'demographic transition' well enough to be sure that it would operate on the universal and permanent lines required by this option.

The other is nine-tenths of what people have in mind when they speak of population control: they mean that a very much wider use of contraception, abortion, and sterilisation has to be facilitated, encouraged, and if necessary enforced. That's how we'll solve the problem if we act briskly enough. Time is short.

But how practical is that option?

Let us look a little more closely at that progressive or serial movement from "facilitated", through "encouraged", to "if necessary enforced". It used to be widely believed that facilitation would be enough. The world's poor, unable to control themselves, were having far more babies than they wanted. They were in fact crying out for contraceptives and the rest, and in justice and charity alike, we in the richer countries had a duty to meet this demand: we should establish clinics in all relevant areas, we would provide the equipment and the training, all at little or no cost, and we could expect full advantage to be taken of this great benefaction. Birth-rates would then fall sharply, and that would relieve the burden of poverty far more effectively than any possible programme of aid and development. Malthus had argued that poverty cannot be relieved, since any increase in food supply must be more than offset by a greater increase in the number of hungry mouths. We have it in our power to prove him wrong, and the only thing needed is facilitation.

But is it?

One of the most interesting happenings at the Bucharest Conference of 1974 was the public recantation of John D. Rockefeller III, who had long been active in that cause and programme. It took place not in the official United Nations Conference but in the associated public Tribune, and like much else at Bucharest, it received remarkably little coverage in the world's press. It was not a recantation of purpose but only of method or strategy. Mr. Rockefeller admitted frankly that facilitation had been tried and was *not* enough. Its effect upon birth-rates was real but very limited: if the desired results were to be attained, there would need to be strong encouragement or (as he put it) "educational and economic incentives".[12]

A cynic might prefer to speak of brain-washing and bribery; and there is something distasteful in that spectacle of an extremely wealthy man requiring the thought and behaviour of the poor to be modified in a sense chosen by himself.

But how much practical realism is there in such hopes? Various writers have dreamed of a Utopian future in which thought-control has caused the large family to seem a shamefully anti-social thing, not only in the eyes of the government but also in the eyes of friends and neighbours: married couples would then produce babies in ones and twos alone, instinctively and as a matter of public decency, very much as they now refrain from copulating in public.

Call that a pretty dream if you like. But how plausible is it? People's external behaviour is capable of being controlled to some extent, and there are techniques of brain-washing. But the large-scale modification of thought is another matter.

Let us consider two very different experiments in that sense. For several generations now, the Soviet government has done its best, by educa-

[12] From my own notes, taken on the spot.

tional and other methods, to make sure that all the people think, talk, write, and behave on soundly Marxist lines. It has achieved considerable success as regards published writing and public behaviour: such things must always be more or less controllable by a sufficiently cruel and arrogant State. But *samizdat* flourishes; and those who know the Soviet Union well are fairly unanimous in telling us that Marxism—as an actually believed faith—is a rarity in that country. Everybody has to pay it lip-service. But few people really believe in it; and if those external controls were lifted, the great majority would immediately embark upon the most shockingly un-Marxist patterns of writing and behaviour. That's after some sixty-odd years of steady indoctrination; and the Party concedes as much by refusing to relax those external controls.

At the opposite extreme, consider the Church. For nearly two thousand years now, it has been persuading people to think and behave as Christians. Yet its instances of total success are rare: we call them 'saints'. Sin and heresy abound, even among those who have been most carefully educated in virtue and true faith.

So with the large-scale lowering of birth-rates by voluntary methods. Facilitation achieves a little, and encouragement only achieves a little more: the necessary revolution in thought and values cannot be caused to happen. Great hopes were expressed—by certain parties—at Bucharest: ten years later, at Mexico City, there was little progress to report.

The brute fact is that in order to be effective, any real programme of population control has to involve compulsion. That puts the emphasis upon abortion and sterilisation, since all methods of contraception depend upon the consent and co-operation of the couple in question. It is well known that China has grasped that nettle. Conversely, at the Mexico City Conference of 1984, the Americans, to their great credit, refused support to any population programme anywhere that involved either abortion or compulsion.

Given the state of their own law and practice, it was perhaps a shade hypocritical of them to take such a stern line against abortion in other countries; and they favoured the general cause of family-planning and population control at both U.N. Conferences, as did the British and all the wealthier countries. But so far as compulsion was concerned, America was there standing up for the finely traditional and democratic value judgment that freedom matters more than immediate well-being.

But how can we resolve the implied contradiction? How can we vote for freedom *and* for population control? In practice, that calls for a kind of large-scale compulsion or coercion which is politically intolerable, morally outrageous, and probably unworkable as well, rather as Prohibition proved unworkable in the United States. The urge to drink liquor is strong, but the reproductive urge is stronger and more universal. If attacked by government, might it conceivably seek the protection of organised crime, as the liquor trade did in dry America? How does one bootleg an illicit baby?

Most people are understandably shy about mentioning the obvious fact that if there is a 'population problem', it might be approached—with far greater practical realism—from the other end.

It is acknowledged on all sides that the 'population explosion' does not stem from any new addiction to the delights of sex and parenthood: it stems, almost entirely, from our new success in keeping people alive; more precisely, in causing babies to survive through childhood and on through the reproductive years of adult life. "The crux is that it is enormously easier to introduce modern methods of death-control than it is to introduce any methods of birth-control."[13] It is indeed, since we go along with instinct in the former case but

[13] Anthony Flew, in his introduction to *An Essay on the Principle of Population*, by Thomas Malthus (London: Penguin Books, 1970), 47, hereafter cited as *Essay*.

against instinct in the latter. We want to be kept alive; and if we are kept alive for long enough, we 'naturally' produce babies in the most shamelessly exponential manner. Death-control thus gives the basic mathematics of Malthus greater scope to operate: always true in theory, it has recently become very much more true in practice.

There have always been anxieties about population, one way or the other, as already observed. For their present and almost eschatological intensity, the thing chiefly responsible is death-control. Was that ever a good thing?

It might well be argued, from certain points of view which are not my own, that it was both morally and practically a thoroughly bad thing. What kind of proud fool is *Homo sapiens*, that he should seek exemption from the evolutionary and eugenic wisdom of Mother Nature, as though he were some kind of superior being and deserved privilege? She provided for 'the survival of the fittest', thereby ensuring the quality of the stock: we have replaced that by the survival of nearly everybody, thus courting a doom of biological degeneration, while also saddling ourselves with a problem that shows no sign of being soluble. What proud folly!

The practical answer is obvious. "Never reinforce failure", says an old military axiom. So we must on no account help the failures of this world—that is to say, the poor and hungry and weak—with economic development and food and running water and soap and sanitation and public health provisions and individual medical attention and so forth. That's what we do now, and it's disastrous: it only causes low-quality people to survive and multiply their low quality lives in that worthless and explosive manner.

I hasten to say that I make no actual recommendation in that sense. But if we ignore all religious considerations and regard *Homo sapiens* as a specialised mammalian species and nothing more, it's hard to see how such a policy can be faulted. Most of us would probably respond with horror to the very idea, as to the most shocking heartlessness. But that would be a gut-reaction rather than a considered judgment: we'd soon get used to the idea, and would need to feel no guilt about doing so, as though such a policy would be *immoral*. There are no moral absolutes, and guilt is only a pathological delusion; or so we are told by many influential philosophers.

Stamp out promiscuous death-control! That's a sound policy in principle, since it tackles the cause of the problem, not merely the symptoms, and it would be cheap and simple and highly effective. The only problem would be that of modifying public opinion so as to eliminate negative gut-reactions. But this would be much easier than in the two cases cited earlier, since we would be modifying people's minds in a highly natural, highly congenial sense. Indifference to other people's problems and sufferings is something that comes all too easily to human nature, whereas it's an uphill task to be a good Christian or a 'good' Communist.

Tongue in cheek, I there offer a really practical answer to the problem. It's certainly a great deal more practical than the wild dream of modifying first the mental processes and then the sexual and reproductive behaviour of an entire mammalian species, universally and permanently and in a sense radically opposed to Nature and all human instinct.

Utopian fantasies are always fun. But they need to be recognised for what they are.

Effective population control, by less draconian methods and without compulsion, should probably be listed among those numerous delusions of power to which affluent and technological and governmental man is chronically prone. Could it ever succeed, except briefly and locally? Its most celebrated propagandist hardly thought so, since he described the chances of success as "infinitesimal",[14] and he appears to have given up even that infinitesimal hope a good many years ago: "When you reach a point where you realize further efforts will be futile, you may as well look after yourself and your friends and enjoy what little time you have left. That point for me is 1972."[15]

Such efforts must always be futile. The reproduction of our species is just about the most private and decentralised of all our activities, while its motivations lie deep in the psychology and physiology of the individual and the couple. It would be hard to imagine an activity—other than thought itself—which would be less amenable to any kind of public planning and control. People do not make love and start babies in order to meet government estimates of required manpower, and they are most unlikely to hold back for any converse reason.

Just before the Bucharest Conference of 1974, the London *Times* spoke in rare tones of sober realism. "The population question . . . should be classified for purposes of political action with the weather. It is something you try to forecast, and as often as not get wrong; something you do not waste time trying to control, but to which you

[14] *The Population Bomb,* 167.

[15] Paul Ehrlich in a magazine interview: *Look*, April 21, 1970.

adapt arrangements and revise plans as the need arises."[16] That contrasts sharply with the almost hysterical doomtalk already instanced.

The latter still continues, if somewhat less stridently, and may soon come upon us once again, perhaps more intensely than ever: it still needs consideration and a diagnosis that should not only be psychological. What kind of thinking lies behind it? What philosophy and what value judgments does it presuppose? And how do these compare with the philosophy and value judgments of a Christian?

[16] Editorial, August 1974.

II

Superfluity and Purpose

Where no effective remedy seems likely to be available, the patient need not necessarily abandon all hope. He should reconsider the disease. Has it been diagnosed correctly? Is it really there at all? Some people, supposing themselves to be mortally sick, are in fact suffering from nothing more substantial than acute hypochondria.

According to a very common diagnosis, this world is an acute case, even a terminal case, of 'over-population': there are, or there soon will be, 'too many people'. A dominant orthodoxy in that sense reigns like an established Church or a totalitarian Party. But like all diagnoses or dominant orthodoxies, it is capable of being questioned, and in two quite separate ways.

There are some who question its factual basis. The trouble is that they usually lie open to charges of *a priori* thinking, religious or ideological. Marxism provides us with a case in point. Successive editions of the *Soviet Encyclopaedia* have told us that in a Socialist country, there can be no such thing as over-population;[17] and at the Bucharest Conference of 1974, the Soviet delegate said that given proper Socialist planning, this world could feed any number of people. His personal embarrassment, as he spoke in that sense, was obvious and gave much amusement. We all knew that Ivan in Moscow would have been hungry at that very moment, were it not for the wickedly Capitalist American bread on his table; and that, after more than half a century of 'proper Socialist planning'. China took the same line at Bucharest but now acts otherwise, illustrating the sad fact already mentioned, that in order to be effective, any population-policy needs to involve compulsion.

Then there are certain Catholics whose optimism takes a different form: "There can't and mustn't be a population problem, since if there were, it would put us Catholics into an impossible position!" That dilemma is a familiar one indeed. If we go along with any kind of population policy, we shall effectively be endorsing practices which our moral tradition has always condemned: if we do not, we shall be accused of heartlessness, of putting legalism before compassion, which is not what Jesus recommended. We seem to face a choice between two possible infidelities.

[17] See *Zero Growth?*, by Alfred Sauvy (Oxford: Basil Blackwell, 1975), 27.

This book is mostly an attempt to show that the dilemma is an unreal one. But it seems real to a great many Catholics and others, and we may therefore come under suspicion of closing our eyes or bending the facts in order to avoid serious challenge. Let some Catholic scholar of high standing write most learnedly about population dynamics and food production: unless his findings are soundly pessimistic, they are likely to be dismissed out of hand by his fellow-scholars in such fields, simply by reason of his religious affiliation.

That dominant orthodoxy about over-population certainly needs to be questioned in factual terms, its basis being less rigorously scientific than is commonly supposed, far more a matter of political and economic and racial self-interest, not to mention the ideological factors which I propose to consider. But that particular task should perhaps be left to scholars without religious affiliation. Catholic scholars may work on it: they can hardly expect to get a fair hearing.

But I propose to question that diagnosis and orthodoxy on totally different lines. The world's acute and possibly terminal disease is commonly named—with great confidence—as 'over-population' or 'too many people'. But is there such a disease? Do those expressions actually *mean* anything? If they turned out to be devoid of meaning, no question of population control could possibly arise.

That may seem like a very fine-spun sort of possibility, even a kind of paradox, and hasty thinkers might respond to it with impatience and contempt. "Those expressions have a perfectly clear meaning! Whatever the facts may be, there must be at least the possibility of over-population, of too many people: when we talk about that possibility, we aren't talking pure gibberish."

We may or may not be. I do not suggest that those two expressions are absolutely and invariably nonsensical. But I do suggest that where they have meaning, they derive it from certain background assumptions or beliefs, philosophical or ideological or religious in nature and often held subconsciously. Given background assumptions of some different sort, they can indeed lose all coherent meaning.

In other words, neither of those two expressions—they are synonymous for all practical purposes—is capable of being strictly and scientifically factual, in the sense of being value-free. Each implies a quantitative value judgment, negative in sense, upon the present or future existence of human beings; and it is clear enough that we cannot derive value judgments of any kind from scientific and statistical facts *alone*. There has to be at least a component within them that comes from somewhere else.[18]

But from where? And of what kind?

So let us cast a searching eye upon this expression 'too many people' and upon the implied value judgments; and by way of clearing the air, let us observe that it is often used loosely, with reference to people's behaviour or location rather than to their existence.

"Too many people smoke cigarettes", we might say with good cause; and we might speak in similar terms of any other activity which we take to be foolish or dangerous or immoral. But we'd be straining language if we said that too many cigarette-smokers *existed*. It's their behaviour that we object to, not the mere fact of their being alive.

We can also object to their location. Anyone who attends cocktail-parties will be familiar with the desperate feeling of "There are too many people in here!" The room is smoke-filled and horribly crowded, conversation is multiplied into uproar: people keep bumping into you, so that your drink is constantly at risk. There are 'too many people' indeed. But once again, it isn't their existence that you object to: it's the fact of their

[18] See *The Abolition of Man*, by C. S. Lewis (London: Geoffrey Bles, 1943).

concentration into a very limited space.

There we have miniature versions of situations that also exist on the grand scale. The individual's cigarette-smoking is comparable to a whole society's practice of industrial and other activities that are environmentally disastrous, though rewarding in the short term: that congested party has its counterpart in the big city with its congested millions. Either way, we can pass adverse judgment with good cause. But this will be passed upon behaviour and location respectively, not upon human existence.

This is a distinction of great importance, since when people speak of 'over-population', close attention will often make it clear that they are using that term rather loosely. What they really have in mind is feckless over-industrialism on the one hand and headlong over-urbanisation on the other. It's in those two areas that the relevant kind of doomtalk finds its greatest plausibility.

Once again, let Paul Ehrlich provide us with an illustration: "Too many cars, too many factories, too much detergent, too much pesticide, multiplying contrails, inadequate sewage treatment plants, too little water, too much carbon dioxide—all can be traced largely to too many people."[19] Anyone who has followed the environmental debate of

[19] *The Population Bomb,* 47.

recent decades will be able to extend that list, and will know that the problems so arising are far from trivial. But with the marginal exceptions of sewage-disposal and water, none of them is a direct function of our numbers. Carbon dioxide in the atmosphere may become a very real problem but is a function of our activities, notably fuel-burning and deforestation: the other problems mentioned by Ehrlich—along with many further problems of broadly the same sort—stem, not from population as such, but from certain kinds of behaviour, unknown until recently and by no means necessary for human well-being. As for water-supply and sewage-disposal, our requirements must always and obviously depend upon our numbers. But neither in the big city nor in the countryside does either call for more than a minute proportion of our total effort and resources: where either creates a problem, it's because we've had other priorities. Beyond that, we should remember that water is something that we never 'consume' in any final way, as we consume (say) oil. We only recycle water, and we always did.

Over-population? The real reference of that expression is often to the environmental folly that stems from rabid consumerism. But instead or as well, it can also be to over-urbanisation, the flight to the big cities. If there is to be talk of bombs, the 'population explosion' will often be more accurately described as the 'urban implosion'.

That's happening very violently indeed, far more rapidly than population growth, not everywhere but in many parts of the world, rich as well as poor. People crowd together; and they then create logistic and environmental problems that hardly existed at all in their wider dispersion. They also create political problems, familiar to imperial Rome, as when the unemployable urban millions, dependent upon government hand-outs for survival, become a revolutionary mob. At the best, they call for a vast increase in non-productive governmental activity and expenditure.[20]

That's happening from Calcutta to Mexico City to Lima, and economic factors such as the breakdown of the rural economy are only partly responsible. Over-urbanisation, like drug-taking, may well need to be included among the self-destructive practices to which our rather idiotic species is psychologically prone: who has not heard some rural teenager sighing with boredom and yearning for the bright lights, the action and excitement of Megalopolis? That might be considered a pathological sort of yearning: yet it's no rarity.

Then—and crucially for many compassionate

[20] See *Only One Earth,* 174, for a brief summary of many findings in this area.

people—there's the sense in which 'too many people' really means 'not enough food'. Our hearts are torn by those pictures of skeletal children in the Third World, and we'd be less than human if they were not.

But how precisely is 'not enough food' the accurate name of a real problem? In defiance of Malthus, we have been told—by someone who ought to know—that while a real food problem does exist, it is a matter not of quantity but of distribution alone. "We have always been able to produce more food than population. The problem is in the distribution of food. There will always be periodic areas of crisis, as is happening now in Africa. But in global terms, no."[21]

That relative optimism is not shared universally, and I place no reliance upon it for purposes of this book. But there is at least a big difference between saying, "The world's food distribution system is very inefficient and cries out for improvement" and saying, "There are—or there soon will be—too many people" in some absolute sense, regardless of their location or behaviour or the imperfection of their systems.

That latter judgment is what lies behind the whole debate, especially in its global version, as

[21] Dr. Rafael M. Salas, Director of UNFPA, just before the Mexico City Conference: *Newsweek* (European edition), August 13, 1984.

represented in those exponential curves that are so widely used to frighten us; and my sole concern is with the values then implied. Strictly speaking, the word 'population' refers to the human race as statistically perceived: in what sense, and with what implications, can we pass adverse value judgments upon this? Most of us agree, perhaps vaguely, that human life is some sort of good thing: instinctively and in general (though with exceptions) we rejoice at every birth and mourn every death. But are there statistical or other limits beyond which human life becomes a *bad* thing?

And 'bad' in what cases? By what measure or criterion?

The language of superfluity or excess is always adversative: 'too many' must always indicate some state of affairs which is perceived as undesirable or bad, in whatever sense and degree.

But in actual usage, language of that sort is logically and almost grammatically incomplete. It points beyond itself, and always—when 'pure' in the sense of referring to superfluous existence—at something in the nature of end or purpose or finality. That may be spelled out, or it may be simply taken for granted, perhaps in some unexamined and even unconscious manner. But it has to be there. An assertion of 'too many' must always presuppose some kind of answer to the question 'too many *for what*?' Where that teleological question is deemed meaningless or unanswerable, the language of superfluity or excess makes no sense at all. Whatever things we're talking about, we cannot make quantitative value judgments upon their existence except on the basis of some notion of what they're for.

It is in fact unusual for such value judgments to be 'pure', in that sense of being concerned with superfluous existence alone. I have observed that 'too many people' often refers to behaviour and location rather than to existence, and that is not an exceptional case: the language of superfluity is full of such obliquities, as a few examples will show.

Consider a man who possesses a hundred shirts, presumably for some reason of vanity. Few of us would hesitate to say that he has 'too many' of them: that is to say, most of them are superfluous to any real need that he can possibly have, and we might ask him to share them out among men who possess no shirts at all. As things stand, with each shirt being used so seldom, they represent a certain waste of resources. But there's no further sense in which we can regard the *existence* of all those shirts as a bad thing. 'Too many shirts' has to be relative to circumstances.

Would it make sense to speak of 'too many cars'?

It certainly would; and when crawling along in the fouled air of an urban rush-hour, I have often found myself wishing that somebody would invent a Pill to stop these smelly monsters from reproducing their kind so abundantly. But strictly speaking, I then object not to their existence but to their excessive concentration within a small area: they then defeat their own chief reason for existing, which is easy mobility. It might be replied that in some wider dispersion, there could still be 'too many' of them, in the sense of causing our limited supplies of oil to be squandered, the atmosphere to be polluted as well. Even then, however, pure existence would not come under judgment. Imagine a world in which cars are widely dispersed and are propelled by some non-polluting and very abundant source of energy: in that improbable situation, 'too many cars' could only mean 'more than can serve any useful purpose'. It could hardly suggest anything more positively bad.

In those two cases, we use the language of superfluity to indicate either pointlessness and waste (those hundred shirts) or else positively undesirable consequences (those gas-guzzling air-polluters in their present congestion): in either case, it is location and use that comes under judgment, not pure existence. And those are two particularly straightforward instances. Shirts and cars are man-made artefacts; and while complex motivations may well be involved, we know why we make them, we know what they're for. We can therefore assess any possible superfluity in relation to purpose: we know what we're talking about.

Things get trickier when we turn to objects and creatures that are not man-made. What sense would it make to speak (for example) of 'too many rats'?

One thing is clear enough: we cannot there define superfluity in relation to purpose, since we don't know what (if anything) rats are *for*. A materialist will say that the language of teleology or purpose is nonsensical when applied to the material universe or to any object or creature within it: nothing that isn't man-made is 'for' anything at all. A Christian might feel that God was moving in a particularly mysterious way when he invented *Rattus norvegicus*.

Nonetheless, the citizens of Hamelin—in Browning's poem—were not the only people to find 'too many rats' a painfully meaningful concept. This case has, in fact, one crucial feature in common with the other two. We don't manufacture rats as we manufacture shirts and cars; they just come along. But like shirts and cars, they then constitute part of our immediate environment:

they make an impact upon human life, and a highly deleterious one. They eat our food, they transmit various diseases, they do untold damage, all in direct proportion to their numbers. If there were only a few of them, we wouldn't worry. But since they multiply rapidly in our cities, we soon reach a point at which we decide that there are 'too many' of them—too many, that is, for human well-being. We then embark upon what must (from their point of view) be called genocidal warfare.

But in so doing, we make an almost teleological assumption about them. The purpose or *raison d'être* of a rat—if it has one—is totally unknown to ourselves. But that doesn't mean that we can say absolutely nothing about it. By implication (such things are seldom spelled out) we can declare it secondary or subordinate to human purposes and human needs. That unspoken principle is invoked whenever we kill a rat, and also, of course, whenever we kill other animals for food.

It is not a self-evident principle, nor is it universally held. The Jains are forbidden to kill any living creature, even a rat: we have our vegetarians in the West, and certain people go in for fuss and agitation about 'animals' rights'. If we took their arguments seriously, we might need to say that rats have just as much right to live, and to enjoy the fruits of the earth, as we ourselves have. How far down the scale should we then go? What about 'bacteria's rights'? At present, we wage remorseless chemical warfare upon God's smallest creatures.

That doesn't bother my conscience. Like most of us, I dissent from certain evolutionary views and agree with Scripture (Gen 1:28) in regarding *Homo sapiens* as different from the other animals in kind and not only in degree: also, as possessing a certain primacy, a lordship or at least a stewardship over the rest of creation. Given that assumption—that mere sanity, it might be said—it doesn't follow that rats exist in order to serve human purposes. But in a negative sense at least, we feel authorised to treat them as though they did.

On that basis, though not otherwise, 'too many rats' is a judgment that we can form and then use as a basis for action. Even then, however, it is not an ontological value judgment. It is not the rats' existence that we object to, but only their location and behaviour as affecting ourselves. If they kept to themselves in remote places, we'd leave them alone, caring nothing for their numbers.

Where purpose is non-existent or unknown and where we ourselves remain unaffected, quantitative value judgments upon existence become absurd. What could it possibly mean to speak of 'too many stars'?

It might make a trivial kind of sense. A small child, told to count the stars, might reasonably complain that there were 'too many' of them—meaning, of course, that the task of counting them would be difficult and unendurably tedious. A bored astronomer might conceivably wish that his subject-matter existed on some less unmanageable scale.

But neither of the two standards already invoked will enable us to make a serious judgment of superfluity upon the starry heavens. The materialist will say that stars resemble rats, but differ from shirts and cars, in that the language of teleology or purpose is there nonsensical. There's nothing which the stars could be too numerous *for*; and for all purposes of possible judgment, a Christian is in exactly the same position. When in poetically devout mood, he will say that the heavens show forth the glory of God: when in more theological mood, he will tell us that the stars, like everything else, exist to serve His unsearchable purposes. But he can say nothing specific about what God's purposes are in that connection, or about how they are better served by the existing quantity of stars than by some larger or smaller quantity that Omnipotence might have seen fit to create.

Then, while we all find the night sky beautiful if untidy, the precise number of the stars is something that has no consequences for ourselves, no impact upon human life and well-being.

That statement calls for slight qualification, not only to spare the feelings of the astrologers. The great *nova* of 1572 had momentous consequences for the history of thought, since it showed that the Ptolemaic *stellatum* was not unchangeable after all and might therefore prove fictitious. Further changes and further discoveries in the starry heavens would certainly excite the astronomers and might have similarly dramatic consequences for our picture of the universe. But unless they were such as to threaten us with cosmic disaster, they would have no more direct importance for the majority. It's all too far away. There can't be 'too many stars' for us, or 'not enough': we don't really care.

There are therefore three different ways in which we can invoke the concept of superfluity. Where shirts and cars and other man-made objects are concerned, we can invoke it with great assurance: we know what we're talking about. Where rats are concerned, also the whole range of natural objects and creatures that affect our lives, we can invoke it with equal assurance in practice, but only on the basis of their difference from ourselves and their subsidiarity of 'purpose' if any, their lack of teleological equality. But where the more distant elements of Nature are concerned—the stars, and all other entities that make no real impact upon our condition—any judgment of superfluity depends upon a known teleology for its coherence. There, purpose may or may not exist: if it exists, it may or may not be known to ourselves.

How does 'too many people' fit into that picture? Can a judgment in that sense be made coherently?

Cars and shirts provide us with a very imperfect analogy. By way of coy euphemism, we might speak of some young couple 'making' a baby: it might be deemed more realistic to say that God or Nature or the Life-Force is actually *making* the baby, using those parents as instruments or factory. We would certainly be straining language if we described that baby as a man-made artefact; and if we insist upon doing so, we shall need to give him (or her) as definable a *raison d'être* as that of a shirt or a car.

In practice, that teleological question will continue to haunt the discussion, however we conduct it and whatever analogy we prefer. The stars give us little help. Human beings affect one another's lives, and powerfully: we are making mutual impacts all the time, sometimes helpfully but often harmfully, and we cannot regard our numbers with distant serene detachment. They *matter*.

What about the rats? "There are too many rats when and where their numbers militate against human well-being": that statement of the case would find general acceptance, with only a minority dissenting. Could we make an exactly parallel statement about ourselves? "There are too many people when and where their numbers militate against human well-being": would that make exactly the same *kind* of sense?

For many of us, it would make obvious and complete sense, leaving nothing further to be said.

But it can't be quite as simple as that. There is doubtful logic, for one thing, in speaking of a biological unity (*Homo sapiens*) exactly as we speak of a biological duality and clash of interests (as between *Rattus norvegicus* and *Homo sapiens*). But if it's bad logic, it's temptingly bad logic, since it enables some people to claim primacy over other people, just as man claims primacy over the other animals, and with more or less similar consequences in practice. Racialism is then the great danger, though there are others. There are undoubtedly some for whom the effective though unconscious meaning of 'too many people' is 'too many black and brown people for the comfort and convenience of white people'—a fact which did much to determine the mood and outcome of the Bucharest Conference of 1974.

But I am not here concerned with ethical and political implications, only with quantitative value judgments as such; and it seems clear that if these are to be coherent, they cannot be based upon a wholly fictitious duality. Throughout this debate, we find a consistent tendency to do exactly that— to speak as though the people who *have* the problem are somehow distinct from the people who *are* the problem, as though 'over-population' threatened the human race from the outside as the rats do: "We were doing quite nicely until They started to come along and make trouble!"

I shall return to this subject later. For the moment, I am concerned only with the insufficiency of the formula just proposed. It needs some modification. If we cannot say "too many of them (aliens, rats) for the well-being of our human selves", can we perhaps say "too many of us for our own well-being"?

Perhaps we can. But we should at least be conscious of the implied teleology. If fully spelled out, our formula will become: "There are too many people when and where our numbers threaten and frustrate our own purpose in existing", a purpose which we define in rather vague terms of 'well-being'.

That ought to bother the materialist, since in his view, the language of teleology or purpose can only be applied to artefacts that are fully and literally man-made—not to rats or stars, nor yet to human beings. (We should note what then follows. If our existence has no real purpose, no possible development can militate against that non-purpose, and 'too many people' becomes a meaningless expression once again.)

In the last analysis, purpose is presupposed by every concept of pure superfluity. We can easily say that 'too many people' are crowded here or there, or engage in one deleterious activity or another. But we can only say that 'too many people' *exist* if their numbers threaten the purpose of their own existence; so we need to know what that purpose is.

There is no escaping the ultimate question of what people are *for*.

Three answers to that question are currently in circulation, and I can see no logical possibility of a fourth. The third can wait for the time being. But the first two dominate the present-day debate about population, being constantly invoked by

people who hardly seem aware of thinking tele-
ologically and who might furiously deny the
charge if it were put to them. "I'm only concerned
with statistics and common-sense!" But either or
both of those two answers (they are not mutually
incompatible) will nearly always turn out to be
lurking unsuspected at the back of the mind.

I want to drag them into the light of day. Each
amounts to a development of that crude concept
'human well-being', the emphasis being social in
the first case and individual in the second.

The trouble is that each depends crucially upon
certain background assumptions of the philosophical or ideological or religious kind; and to
speak mildly, these are capable of being called into
question.

III

The Farmer's Cattle

"We are put into the world in order to be of service to others, and to society at large."

That's one answer to the question of what people are for, and in that version, it has religious implications: 'service to others' is what God—or some comparable agent—had in mind when creating us. Some such view is echoed in just about every ethical and moral system, notably in the 'Love your neighbour' of the Old Testament and the New. We should live for others; and in so doing, we shall find the best sort of self-fulfillment there is.

So perhaps we can define the purpose or end or finality of each individual's existence in terms of extrinsic or social usefulness. Most of us do have some such usefulness, since we are of some economic value to society, some emotional value to friends and relatives, and so forth. Shall we find our *raison d'être* in making the most of all that?

We certainly should make the most of it: nobody argues about that duty, nobody admires the

man who is selfish or—not quite the same thing—
self-centred. But ideological questions arise as
soon as we define our *raison d'être* in terms of that
duty, hoping thereby to give 'too many people' a
clear-cut meaning. As before, we shall have to ask
'too many for what?'; and the answer will have to
be 'too many for the good of society' or 'for the
common good'.

That may sound like an obvious common-sense
sort of answer. But its implications need to be
watched. For one thing, it tempts us to a false
duality once again. If we postulate some real or
hypothetical situation in which there are 'too
many people for the good of society', we shall be
drawing a wholly fictitious distinction between
'society' and 'the people who comprise that
society'—in whatsoever numbers—at some particular time. There is no separate and superior
entity called 'society': that word only refers to
people, as perceived in a certain way.

The trouble is that where such an abstract entity
is postulated, as it often is, it becomes an end to
which actual people are only the means. Such an
order of priorities is commonplace, even normal,
in the thought of those who call for population
control. This, we are told by a writer already
quoted, "is the conscious regulation of the numbers of human beings to meet the needs not just of

individual families, but of society as a whole."[22] Society is the end: people are the means, only to be admitted into the world insofar as they serve that end.

Such thinking recurs constantly. "The things that make family planning acceptable are the very things that make it ineffective for population control. By stressing the right of parents to have the number of children they want, it evades the basic question of population policy, which is how to give societies the number of children they need. By offering only the means of couples to control fertility, it neglects the means for societies to do so."[23]

Such writers often slip into the language of commerce, as though 'over-population' were simply a matter of supply exceeding demand. The answer is obvious: you just cut back on production. That's fine where things or possessions are concerned. But are human beings *things*? And if they are possessions, *whose* possessions are they?

The totalitarian implications of such thinking ought to be obvious enough. But many writers are not thereby discouraged from seeing 'population policy' as something to be governed by a sort of cost/benefit analysis, made by 'society' in

[22] *The Population Bomb,* Prologue.
[23] Kingsley Davis, as quoted in *The Population Bomb,* 83.

economic terms, even in simply financial terms. Of the less developed countries, for example, we are told that "a birth control programme is often the most profitable of all possible investments."[24] So also at Mexico City in 1984, where the American delegate, James Buckley, said that "population growth could become an asset or a problem depending on other factors such as. . . ."[25] 'Society' draws up a kind of balance-sheet: people appear on it as assets or liabilities, according to circumstances.

The frequently recurring word 'policy' should remind us that in all such contexts, the effective meaning of 'society' is invariably 'government'—usually national, sometimes local or international.

This fact is often concealed by a number of coy euphemisms. We find it suggested, for example, that the agent of population control will be a mysterious entity which is sometimes called 'we' and sometimes 'Man'. I have already quoted a writer who says that 'we' can 'survive', but only "if we act now. The choice lies in our hands."[26] But *who* is to do the acting and choosing? "Man can still choose his limits and stop when he pleases by

[24] *Essay*, Introduction, 42.
[25] London *Times*, August 10, 1984.
[26] *People Populating*, 355.

weakening some of the strong pressures that cause capital and population growth, or by instituting counterpressures, or both."[27] But when did monolithic 'Man' ever choose to do anything at all? "For the past two centuries population has continued to press on food resources, but today the lid has blown off, and the population growth rate has escaped *control*."[28] But when did 'we' or 'Man' ever control it?

There's a rock-bottom sense in which 'we' always did, individually but not collectively. Babies are not begotten by graphs and trends and statistics: each one comes into existence by reason of a particular action, totally chosen and free on the male side at least, and broadly understood by nearly all of us. In that sense, birth and population were always under human control.

But the thing now demanded is collective control, which—in practice—has to mean control by the government. That, unlike 'society', really is distinct from the people of some given area: it has its own interests and purposes, and only extreme political naivety will suppose that these invariably (or even very frequently) coincide with 'the common good' as ideally conceived. The value or desirability of human existence is thus to become

[27] *Limits to Growth*, 153.
[28] *People Populating*, 42, emphasis added.

conditional, subject to assessment by politicians and bureaucrats.

That assessment need not always be negative. "In South America there are no countries with more than 50 people per square mile. Some of their governments feel that only rapidly rising population will enable them to fill up their national boundaries, achieve the 'critical mass' of producers and consumers needed for a modern economy, or produce the number of citizens needed for prestige, power, and successful national statehood."[29] But while it's bad enough to say that more people *should* exist for such squalidly political purposes as those, it's even worse—and far more common—to invoke similar criteria for saying that they should *not*. "Countries which consider their population growth rate detrimental to national purposes are invited to consider setting population growth targets."[30] It's clear that for 'countries' we must there read 'governments', and for 'national purposes', 'governmental interests'. So also and more candidly: "Although family planning is widely accepted—only two countries prohibit it and many governments now actively promote it—

[29] *Only One Earth,* 216-17.

[30] One of the recommendations submitted to the Mexico City Conference in 1984: see *Population,* the UNFPA newsletter, April 1984.

fertility levels continue to be higher or lower than governments wish and family planning targets are often not met."[31]

How insubordinate the common people are! How imperfectly they trust Big Brother, how contumaciously they behave as though they knew their own best interests and were entitled to make their own decisions! One of the most unpleasant features of this entire debate is the constantly recurring note of managerial interference, of bossiness, even of the imperialist or colonialising mentality: here though not elsewhere, it is still deemed tolerable for the poor benighted savages to be pushed around—in their own interest, of course—by their enlightened betters.

The temptation to play God in other people's lives is a powerful one, especially in government-people, but in all of us to some degree. "Even the most unselfish well-off persons think they know better than do poor people what is good for them and for the world. Most of us secretly harbour the notion that we know how some others should live their lives better than they themselves know. But the thought is only a matter of concern when it is hitched up with sufficient arrogance and wilfulness that we are willing to compel them to do what

[31] Dr. Rafael M. Salas at a press conference: *Population,* April 1984.

we think they ought to do."[32] The London *Times* spoke in similar terms at the time of the Mexico City Conference in 1984: "It would be a pity if statistical man took over from real human beings, to the point where it came to be accepted doctrine within development economics that the pursuit of an increased standard of living was more important than whether or not to raise children. That kind of question must surely be left to parents themselves, without the suspicion that the gentleman in the World Bank—or in any other western institution for that matter—knows better what is good for a Bangladeshi couple than they know themselves."[33] In the same context, we were warned against "a double standard and a contempt for the societies in the less developed world which is often only too close to the surface when the question of world population is discussed in the developed countries".

We should not play God in other people's lives.

All of us attribute some kind of value to the human individual as such. But do we see that value in *wholly* extrinsic and social terms?

If we do, we shall have to declare some people valueless. It is no rare thing for a man or woman to be unproductive, unloved, unhappy, and alone, so

[32] *The Ultimate Resource,* 323.
[33] Leading article, August 10, 1984.

that his death or hers would come as no loss to anybody at all. In such a case, are we to speak of an altogether valueless life?

Our behaviour, if only at moments of crisis, is such as to suggest that most of us still think otherwise. What with fires and shipwrecks and airline crashes and other disasters, situations often arise in which people will die unless rescued; and we take it for granted—quite instinctively—that they *must* be rescued if possible, at whatever cost in time and effort and resources. We seldom or never ask whether the rescue operation is going to be cost-effective, or whether the individuals at risk are economically productive or socially valuable or otherwise worth preserving in some positive way. We normally feel that they have to be rescued, simply because they're human beings: we instinctively attach to the individual human life—merely as such—a value which is absolute, in the sense of being unquantifiable though not exactly infinite.

At a moment of sudden disaster, of course, we seldom have time for any possible evaluation. In more leisured circumstances—in geriatric care, for example—the concept of 'a life that is socially valueless and therefore not worth preserving' finds an increasingly secure foothold in the modern mind, as is shown by the social acceptance of abortion and the steady pressure for euthanasia.

All that follows naturally enough, once we define the purpose or *raison d'être* of human life in terms of social utility alone. "People exist in order to serve others, in order to serve the good of society": that sounds a splendidly unselfish thing to say, a plea for altruism. But unless supplemented from elsewhere, it's a formula for totalitarianism. There are so many people who, on that reckoning, should not be existing at all. Society or Big Brother doesn't want them: they're useless.

Malthus grasped that nettle. "A man who is born into a world already possessed, if he cannot get subsistence from his parents on whom he has a just demand, and if society does not want his labour, has no claim of *right* to the smallest portion of food, and, in fact, has no business to be where he is. At Nature's mighty feast there is no vacant cover for him. She tells him to be gone, and will quickly execute her own orders, if he do not work upon the compassion of some of her guests. If these guests get up and make room for him, other intruders immediately appear demanding the same favour. The report of a provision for all that come, fills the hall with numerous claimants. The order and harmony of the feast is disturbed, the plenty that before reigned is changed into scarcity; and the happiness of the guests is destroyed by the spectacle of misery and dependence in every part of the hall, and by the clamorous importunity of those who are unjustly enraged at not finding the provision which they had been taught to expect."[34]

On any such basis as that, 'too many people' comes to mean 'too many poor people for the comfort and convenience of the rich'; and that's the rock-bottom meaning which the expression does carry for many present-day thinkers, though always by concealed implication. Nobody wants to *say* anything as outrageous as that; and even at the time of Malthus, that passage aroused such indignation that it was omitted from later editions of the *Essay*.

But the concept of 'people who, being socially useless, should not be existing at all' is far from dead. "The untrained worker is not an addition to a productive labour force or to a lively consumer market. He produces so little that even his minimal consumption represents an economic loss. He makes no contribution to his country's growth or strength. On the contrary, he becomes yet another pitiful 'marginal man' stranded on the edge of a less than productive agricultural system or joining the ranks of the unemployed in the squatter fringes of big cities."[35] The social value of such a man is

[34] *Essay*, 1798: quoted in *Zero Growth?*, 24.
[35] *Only One Earth*, 218-19.

zero or negative: how much better if the wretched fellow didn't exist at all! In the same spirit, another writer once asked us to consider "the number of additional people we can value,"[36] with the clear implication that others, surpassing that number, would have to be deemed valueless.

But *which* others?

Here, once again, we encounter a duality and distinction which is logically and factually absurd but which nonetheless appeals strongly to the uglier side of human nature. In the passage just quoted, Malthus asks us to imagine a prosperous humanity dining in comfort until a poor man intrudes upon it from the outside with his impertinent demand to be fed. But he never intruded: he was part of humanity from the start, as were those others.

Population is always an Us: whatever the figures may be, whatever the problems, it's never a separate and threatening It or Them. If we speak of 'over-population', we can only refer to the entire human race, as subjected to a statistically adverse judgment today or in some possible future. Assuming that to be a bad state of affairs, the blame for it has to be shared universally: the guilt of culpably superfluous existence is shared in equal measure by one and all.

[36] William Pratt of the National Center for Health Statistics, *American Ecclesiastical Review,* 166 (1972): 262.

But in practice, that democratic conclusion is seldom reached. Most of us follow Malthus in making that duality and distinction and in putting the blame fairly and squarely upon Them—upon the underprivileged, that is. Those are the value-less, the unwanted, the superfluous ones.

Population control was always a cause of the rich;[37] and while it was not the precise cause to which Malthus devoted his efforts, he very definitely did write in defence of the English class-system as then existing, within which he himself held a secure upper-middle-class position. The passage just quoted is suffused with implications of class-interest and class-conflict, such as still continue to govern all present-day discussions that are more centrally about population control. At every point—notably at Bucharest—it's as though rich people were saying: "I wish the poor would cease to embarrass us by existing in such useless and unsightly and unmanageable quantities!"

But while that's a natural response of wealth, it's also a natural response of arrogant governmental power. We like to distinguish those regimes which are totalitarian from those which are not. But that is a distinction of degree, not of kind. All

[37] In this connection, much amusing testimony will be found in *Breeding Ourselves to Death,* by Lawrence Lader (New York: Ballantine Books, 1971).

government seeks to be absolute and will become absolute in fact unless restrained by effective checks and balances: nominally the servant of the sovereign people, it naturally tends to become their manager and manipulator, even their owner.

So, while population control is partly a cause of the rich against the poor, it's also a cause of government against the citizen. Where poverty continues, witness is borne to the very limited competence of government, to the unwelcome fact that it does not really have a God-like power to solve all problems and provide all good things; and in any case, what farmer wants to have more cattle than he can manage comfortably?

Managerial ownership: that's a key concept for the whole of this debate.

But are we only the State's cattle? All purely social understandings of 'too many people' involve value judgments and background assumptions of that totalitarian sort. Society or the collective or the government is seen as the end: individual existence is seen as a means to that end *and nothing more*. Extrinsic or social value becomes the one-and-only *raison d'être* of the potential human being, and where that seems likely to be zero or negative he must be denied actual existence. The possibility that he might have some further *raison d'être* is excluded on principle.

He then suffers no personal injustice, of course,

since he isn't there to suffer it; and despite various ominous signs, we have not yet gone very far towards the point at which innocent people—guiltless of crime—are considered disposable because their extrinsic or social value is deemed to be zero or negative. (So far, we only give that treatment to unborn children. But we are starting to give it to newly born children who turn out to be malformed or otherwise defective, and it's unlikely that the senile and the insane and the incurable will have very long to wait.)

But I am not here concerned with courses of action, only with the value judgments that precede them, especially those involved in that purely social understanding of 'too many people'. There's a tremendous ethical difference between our treatment of potential and of actual people, and not even the most punctilious of Catholics will now maintain that contraception—when accurately so called—is the same sin as homicide,[38] though a negative judgment upon human life is implied in either case.

So on the larger scale. Nobody yet proposes that

[38] The two were often linked in mediaeval times, but only as a matter of classification, based upon very imperfect knowledge of reproductive physiology. It was never a matter of *inference*, from the supposedly homicidal character of contraception to an immorality of which it would not otherwise have been suspected.

the 'population problem' should be resolved by a policy of culling, of selective massacre, though just such a policy was recommended in various quarters in the aftermath of the French Revolution:[39] the great massacres and genocides of this century were not motivated by strictly demographic considerations.

Ethically speaking, such a programme and policy would differ sharply from what we find advocated today. But the underlying value judgment would be identical. Either way, we invoke the concept of a human life that's socially useless or deleterious and is superfluous and undesirable on that account, having no further *raison d'être* whatever.

That's a totalitarian concept in itself, no matter whether present or future lives are being discussed.

[39] See *Zero Growth?*, 21.

IV

Worthless Existence

"What are human beings for?" If we answer that question in solely extrinsic or social terms, we shall be making ideological presumptions of the ugliest sort.

What will happen if we answer it in other terms, intrinsic or individual? What if we reject all totalitarianism and assert firmly that each person is an end in himself, that government is only a means and 'society' an unreal abstraction?

We shall be in various sorts of trouble at once. For one thing, we shall be in danger of erecting individualism into an absolute, whereas man is a social animal and is universally recognised to have social duties. We shall also come close to self-contradiction. If each individual is an end absolutely, serving no purpose beyond himself, he isn't 'for' anything at all. He just exists as the stars do, and the concept of 'too many people' becomes null and void once again. We have answered the question by declaring it to have no answer.

That non-answer has its plausibility and (for some) a kind of attraction, the idea of a wholly pointless and purposeless existence being urged upon us, in the name of objectivity or realism, by certain existentialists and other philosophers of despair. But most of us find it unendurable. There has to be something more than mere existence, there has to be something to live for!

Strictly speaking, of course, strong feelings in that sense prove nothing. Many aspects of reality are more or less 'unendurable'—one's own mortality, for example—while still needing to be endured. Those who attribute existential absurdity to all human life are (in my view) mistaken. But it's more to the immediate point that their voice, if given a hearing, will simply terminate the present discussion. 'Too many people' will become as meaningless as everything else. No value judgment can be passed upon the totally pointless, the existentially absurd.

Let us therefore proceed on the more congenial assumption that from the individual's point of view, there must indeed be something more than mere existence, something to live for.

What can that be? For the time being, let us refrain from defining it in religious terms. It then becomes curiously undefinable. What *are* we living for? Or, in slightly different terms: what do we *hope* for? Happiness? Well-being? Self-fulfilment?

A high-quality life? For convenience, let's settle for 'happiness', always remembering the word's inadequacy, also its extreme philosophical and psychological difficulty.

Have we now reached an answer? "Human beings exist for individual happiness": that formula expresses one perfectly natural instinct of the human mind, often encountered in discussion with the less sophisticated. "*What are we here for? We're here to enjoy life, to have a good time if we can: where's the problem?*" Insofar as we agree, we can give a seemingly clear meaning to the expression 'too many people': human numbers are excessive when and where they militate against individual happiness.

But ambiguity lurks in every such statement of the case. Are we then referring to the *sum total* of all human happiness, or to the *average* happiness of individuals everywhere?

That may seem a somewhat unreal distinction, since happiness cannot be quantified very easily or very realistically, while "the sum total of all human happiness" is experienced by nobody. It is a distinction that we need to draw, nonetheless. Its difficulty is that of a famous concept which Jeremy Bentham took over from Francis Hutcheson, "the greatest happiness of the greatest number". Something of that sort is implied in all assertions that over-population can militate against individual happiness. But can we really think of maximising two such variables at the same time?

Let us think of 'happiness' as comprising a number of possible 'satisfactions'. Not all of these will be quantifiable, but longevity certainly is; and although Evelyn Waugh once described it as a curse, inflicted upon us by the wicked doctors, most of us consider it desirable, a good thing, a definite 'satisfaction'. Few people want to die young.

Now let us consider two cases. In the first, there are a hundred people who live to the ripe old age of ninety: in the second, there are three hundred people who die at thirty. Which case comes closer to Bentham's ideal? The totality of life, to be enjoyed or endured as the case may be, is nine thousand person/years in either case. Can we judge between them?

We might play a similar game with food requirements, though these are rather less precisely quantifiable than longevity. It is certainly a 'satisfaction' to be well fed, and malnutrition is only sought by ascetics. But which is better—a small number of well-fed people, or a larger number of undernourished people?

So with all possible 'satisfactions' and with 'happiness' itself, though our quantification will have to be highly subjective at many points. The question is a perfectly real one, since "the greatest happiness of the greatest number" can be understood in two ways, one particular answer to it—a highly controversial answer—being usually taken for granted by those who call for population control.

In the first chapter of this book, I mentioned a conspicuous tendency to speak of over-population in terms of eschatological doom and final collapse. In more temperate language, the situation thus envisaged might be described as one in which, while human numbers have increased sharply, the average satisfaction-level of the individual has declined—rather less sharply, perhaps, or rather more sharply.

But by Bentham's standard, would that be a better or a worse situation than what we have today? Let us agree, in general terms, that we want the world to contain as much human happiness as possible: in that day of doom and collapse, there might well be more of it than there is now. Individuals might have less of it, but there would be more of them to have it.

In practice, calculations of that sort are out of the question, partly because there are too many economic and other unknowns, and partly because happiness cannot really be quantified. I make this rather fanciful suggestion of a cost/benefit analysis—one that cannot actually be made—in order to draw attention to the complexity of the question. "Human numbers are excessive when and where they militate against individual happiness": that may seem like a simple and obvious statement of the case. In fact, it's decidedly ambiguous.

And if we want to invoke it as the basis for some policy of population control, we shall need to make a jump which is often made but seldom recognised for what it is. Given this present emphasis upon the individual, we shall need to say that it's somehow better to have *no satisfactions at all*—not even the satisfaction of mere existence—than to have low-level satisfactions alone, as when one lives hungry and dies young.

Throughout this debate about population, value judgments in that sense are expressed again and again—sometimes explicitly, often in some oblique but unmistakable fashion—by people who seem unaware of their controversial implications. We all prefer a reasonably 'high-quality' sort of life, with a fair availability of some satisfactions at least, especially the basic (and related) satisfactions of food, health, and longevity. But are we to say that the inescapably 'low-quality' life—characterised by malnutrition, sickness, and early death—is simply *not worth living at all?* that few and meagre satisfactions are *worse* than none?

That needs to be recognised as a metaphysical and religious question, far beyond Bentham's reach. It concerns the relationship between two ultimate concepts, 'being' and 'goodness'.

Is mere existence a 'satisfaction'?

Many people would say that it's nothing of the sort, that it's only the precondition of all possible satisfactions. "It's good to be alive!", we might say upon occasion, but imprecisely: we would then be referring to the blissful satisfactions of some exceptional moment, not to existence as such.

Or would it be nearer the mark to say that the bliss of such exceptional moments draws our attention to the inherent goodness of *all* existence?

A relevant distinction found its way into the popular speech of my younger days. Where some condition or life-style seemed unendurably tedious or otherwise 'low-quality', certain people would say "That isn't living—that's just *existing!*" In much the same way, the Chorus in Eliot's *Murder in the Cathedral* repeatedly describe themselves as "living and partly living". They are poor housewives, their satisfactions are few.

A great many of us speak and write as though human existence had no point or purpose that was not conferred by satisfactions, economically definable and needing to grow progressively richer and more abundant throughout the foreseeable future. Rising 'standards of living' are what matters. If we faced some long-term and inescapable decline into poverty—into mere existence—there would be no point in going on at all.

We find very similar judgments expressed in connection with population, as by one editor of Malthus: "Once we firmly raise our aims above mere subsistence and towards the achievement and maintenance of prosperous standards of living, then it becomes fairly easy to demonstrate the need for checks on fertility."[40] "Subsistence" there has the adversative sense of 'existing' in that old-fashioned idiom, and it indicates something that isn't enough. Getting richer: that's what life is all about, and quantity must be sacrificed to 'quality' as so conceived. There's no point in the low-quality life.

That presumption recurs constantly throughout all discussions of population. When the World Population Plan of Action was being discussed at Bucharest, the Brazilian delegate said very pertinently: "The plan and supporting documents take for granted that life is not worth living, other than

[40] *Essay* (Introduction), 42.

on terms of very high energy-consumption and material comfort."[41] It did indeed, going far beyond what most of us would say. But a great many of us would say the same thing in a less extreme version, as though low standards of material comfort really did cause the individual's life to be more or less worthless for himself as well as for society.

The curious thing is that such value judgments get little serious attention, as was observed by one writer. "Some economists and laymen believe that some people's lives are so poor that they would be better off had they never been born. Others believe that no life is so poor that it does not have value. Still others believe that only the individual should be allowed to decide whether his or her own life is worth living. Surprisingly to me, this value, which is one of the most influential in population discussions, is rarely mentioned explicitly."[42]

One might ask how *expertise* in economics or in anything else—with the possible exceptions of philosophy and theology—qualifies anyone to speak of such matters with more authority than the rest of us. Ideally, therefore, one might expect the specialised expert to adopt one of two possible options. In the first place, he might preface his

[41] From my own notes, taken on the spot.
[42] The *Ultimate Resource,* 334.

work on population with a brief religious or anti-religious or philosophical or ideological statement: the reader, being thus warned, would know how to understand any subsequent value judgments and allow for their possibly deceptive influence. Alternatively, the writer might subject himself to a rigorous discipline of factual objectivity, carefully avoiding even the most implicit sort of value judgment. He might then give us (for example) a full clinical account of malnutrition in all its tragic stages. But if he had personal feelings about the point at which the undernourished life becomes valueless, he would keep them strictly to himself, giving his readers no hint.

But the rigorous observance of either discipline is a rarity. It is usual for writers about population to form their own judgments about this very basic question—the value of a human life to its possessor—and then to slip these into their otherwise factual analyses, as though they were either manifest axioms or else academically established certainties, beyond all reasonable criticism.

Examples abound: let one suffice. It is usual for a book to end with some statement that is central to its purpose, since last words are emphatic and linger in the reader's memory. It is therefore noteworthy that *Limits to Growth* ends on just such a note of unwarranted judgment. "The crux of the matter is not only whether the human race will

survive, but even more whether it can survive
without falling into a state of *worthless* existence."[43] The writers were able people in their
various specialised fields: did they feel competent,
for that reason, to decide the level of 'quality'
below which human existence becomes 'worthless'?

The sad fact is that fortunate people have a
marked tendency to see theirs as the only tolerable
sort of existence. It's as though two propositions
added up to a third. "*I* wouldn't want to live in that
wretched condition!" That's understandable
enough. "I am offended and disgusted by the spectacle of people who do live in that wretched condition!" That's understandable too, if morally unpleasant. But no kind of logic will then enable us to
say, "Life in that wretched condition is simply
worthless: they'd be better off without it."

The danger of such bias is perhaps inescapable,
since books about population are seldom written
by people who actually do live in extreme poverty.
(It is not only books. The Bucharest Conference
dealt extensively with poverty, and someone re-
marked that not one single poor person spoke
from first to last, nor was one even present.) But
that bias needs to be recognised and allowed for. In
June 1984, Robert McNamara told the world that

---

[43] *Limits to Growth,* 197, emphasis added.

population had not ceased to be a pressing problem: it threatened us with a frightening increase of "absolute poverty", that being his term for living conditions "so characterised by malnutrition, illiteracy, and disease as to be beneath any reasonable definition of human *decency*".[44] That was an unconsciously revealing choice of words. Decency, like its opposite, is in the eye of the beholder: the indecent is that which offends other people.

If we are to speak of the valueless life, we must be careful about who does the judging, and by what standards. We might even ask the people concerned. Suicide is the most concrete assertion that life has been found worthless: it correlates with certain kinds of unhappiness, but hardly at all with poverty as such, even with very great poverty. At the other extreme, we have all met malformed or otherwise handicapped people who would have qualified for abortion by present-day standards—"If we allow this foetus to live, it can only have a worthless existence!"—but who manage to cope with their problems and enjoy life thoroughly.

It's proud and tyrannical to pass adverse judgment upon the intrinsic worth of someone else's

44 *Newsweek* (European edition), June 25, 1984, emphasis added.

existence. He may offend us, society may not want him. But he may quite possibly want himself.

If he never comes into existence, of course, 'he' won't miss what he has never enjoyed.

I have already hinted at the paradox to which those quotation marks draw attention. *Who* won't miss what he has never enjoyed? It is a paradox into which we may pardonably slip in the course of casual conversation, and readers of *Emma* will remember Isabella Knightley's comment upon the childlessness of the ill-tempered Mrs. Churchill: "What a blessing, that she never had any children! Poor little creatures, how unhappy she would have made them!" We see what she meant. But we need not waste many tears on the sufferings of those poor little creatures. Even in the already fictitious world of the novel, their existence is entirely hypothetical, and they cannot be made unhappy.

Comparable assertions are often made in connection with population, as was observed in a passage already quoted: "Some economists and laymen believe that some people's lives are so poor that they would be better off had they never been born."[45] *Who* would be better off?

It should be clear that when we are attempting to think rigorously, we must avoid all such literally nonsensical assertions. A 'person' who remains totally hypothetical—who is not born or even

[45] *The Ultimate Resource,* 334.

conceived, who never comes into any sort of existence at all—cannot strictly be said to gain or lose by any possible turn of events.

That obvious truth has momentous consequences for 'too many people', insofar as that concept relates to individual well-being. We have already considered the case in which certain potential lives are expected to be socially undesirable and are excluded from actuality on that account: that involves the totalitarian assumption that social utility is our one-and-only *raison d'être*. But what of the life which is expected to be a bad thing *for the person concerned* and must therefore be prevented for 'his' own sake? We cannot really say that birth would remove 'him' from blessed non-existence, in which 'he' is far better off. If such judgments are to be made at all, they will have to invoke the concept of human existence—in sufficiently adverse circumstances—being a *positive evil*.

Can there be such a thing as that? A good question; and what needs great emphasis is the fact that it takes us into the realm of metaphysics and religion. It is not a question which anybody can answer with confidence on the basis of his *expertise* in demography and the other social sciences.

The relationship between being and goodness has teased mankind from the beginning, and it has been seen in broadly three ways.

In the first place, there are certain metaphysical and religious positions from which our life in this world can be declared either illusory or else positively evil in itself, no matter what its 'quality' may be: our only real hope then lies in the soul's liberation from its present jailhouse of corrupted flesh. For convenience, I shall refer to that as a 'Manichaean' view of the human condition, though the particular cult that stemmed from Mani was only one of its numerous and highly influential versions. It offers one sort of answer to the problem of theodicy, and it necessarily separates any idea of 'God' from the idea of creation.

At the other extreme, we find those two ideas bracketed very closely together, even to the point of identification, as by the Christians. It then follows—however mysteriously—that all being or existence, as such, is good, and that 'evil' is a strictly negative concept. There can be no such thing as a positive evil; and in particular, every human life—no matter what degree of hardship it may involve—possesses an inherent or ontological goodness or value which, if not precisely infinite, is certainly unquantifiable.

Then there's a middle position, adopted more or less instinctively by a great many people, including some Christians of the less consistent sort. On this reckoning, while human life is often or usually a good thing for its possessor, extremes of hardship can make it into a positive evil *for him*, though perhaps not in the sight of God. To say the least, that idea of 'a positive evil' cannot be ruled out on principle (what about Auschwitz? what about cancer?) and to that extent, the Christians are wrong. But the Manichees are wrong as well, since there's a great deal of good in most people's experience.

Any man is at liberty to think like that. But I want to stress the fact that he will then be adopting a metaphysical and religious position, and a highly controversial one. Too many of us assume too easily that the whole question of population is essentially objective and scientific, not totally value-free perhaps, but involving no judgments more controversial than 'extreme poverty should be relieved if possible'. So if we get the facts from the relevant experts, they will provide us with a sufficient basis for policy.

But facts alone can never do that. Before we move on from fact to policy, we have to pass through the crucial intermediate stage of value judgment; and it's logically and even grammatically impossible to answer questions of value—of moral value especially, of righteous and benevolent action—by appealing to fact and science alone. Premises that are strictly in the indicative can never generate conclusions in the imperative or even the optative. Other considerations will be involved in our policy decision; and whether we like it or not, whether we recognise it or not, these will be metaphysical or religious (or of course anti-religious) in nature.

They need to be spelled out and squarely faced. Where anything as basic as human existence is concerned, and the possibility of its being 'useless' or 'a positive evil', the underlying presumptions need far more attention than they get.

There are various philosophies of despair. But in the present-day West, very few people are prepared to say, fairly and squarely, that our life in this world is evil in itself, that every birth is a disaster. Theologies of the Manichaean sort have been very influential in the European past: they survive, and powerfully, but mostly in the attenuated form of moods and sentiments, very seldom as fully-worked-out and conscious belief-systems.

So when it comes to the possibility of human life being an inherently evil thing, a disaster to be prevented if possible, few if any of us will say that it *always* has that quality. But the third of the three options just mentioned is a popular one: a great many will say that in circumstances of great poverty and hardship, life does become a positive evil, whatever the Christians may say.

That's different in theory from a fully Manichaean position. But it comes fairly close to that in practice.

We who are well-fed and live the 'high-quality' life, as currently understood in the West, can easily forget the exceptional nature of our present condition. We like to feel that life is naturally comfortable, or can be made so at least, though doubtlessly with just a few anomalous cases of inescapable hardship. Yes, there are desperately poor people in the Third World, and their life isn't really worth living at all. But given a little goodwill and the right political and economic policies, they can be helped, if not into affluence, then at least into some sort of tolerably worth-while existence.

But our adverse judgment is not then passed upon the present life-style (and death-style) of an exceptionally unfortunate few: it is passed upon the vast bulk of human existence everywhere, in the past and—quite possibly—in the future as well. The comforts known to you and me are exceptional, and we have no guarantee of their permanence.

Whatever the future may hold in store for us, the poor and generally 'low-quality' life has always been the historically and geographically normal thing for *Homo sapiens*. Let us say, if we must, that it isn't worth living. But we shall then be saying that with rare and local and perhaps temporary exceptions, human existence over these countless millennia has been a positive evil, a curse, a misfortune.

That might be called a qualified Manichaeanism.

A related but distinct version of that ancient *Weltanschauung* becomes manifest as well, in the course of many discussions of population, but as a gut-feeling rather than an intellectual position. It's one thing to argue that human life can be a positive evil and has mostly been exactly that: it's slightly different, but not totally different, to express a powerfully emotional revulsion from it, in one's own case or in others. Comment needs to be philosophical or theological in the former case, psychological in the latter.

Such a revulsion appears in different versions. I have already mentioned the embarrassed distaste with which wealth naturally looks upon poverty, as upon something indecent; and beyond that, we often encounter a deep-seated hatred of human fertility as such. Those who have taken part in the relevant controversies will have often found that hatred taking an anti-Catholic form: "They breed like rabbits!"—as though there were something disgusting in the reproductive behaviour of *Lepus cuniculus*. We have there an instance of what may

loosely be called 'puritanism', a phenomenon of
great psychological interest, manifested in many
literary and artistic areas as well as in theology: it
seems to be what causes so many of us to extend a
joyous welcome to all this doomtalk about population, as justifying a war against Venus which they
already desired to wage for private reasons of their
own.[46]

But there's something else as well, something
very real though seldom articulated—our general
self-hatred, individual and collective.

Every clinical psychiatrist has met this in its
individual version. It has nothing to do with what
Christians call 'humility' or 'remorse' or 'repent-
ance'. It's far less moralistic, far more existential
than that: it's about what we are, not what we do.
We hate ourselves for our own humanity, and on
this statistical pretext among others.

Consider the language used in this connection.
'Population' only means 'people, as statistically
considered'. But that's something nasty. It's a
bomb, an imminent explosion, a menace: it's a
pollution, a curse, a plague, a cancer, a monster, an
octopus, almost a devil.[47] Paul Ehrlich saw fit to

[46] See Appendix, 4.
[47] See *The Ultimate Resource,* 311, for many references;
but terminology of more or less that sort prevades the entire
literature.

begin *The Population Bomb* with a highly emotional vision of urban poverty in India, and he
spoke as one confronted not so much by misfortune as by a disgusting and almost obscene pullula-
tion.

Whenever we consider value judgments upon
human existence (as distinct from human well-
being) we must allow for the fact that at certain
murky depths, we hate ourselves and one another
as well, individually and collectively, with little
discrimination. All talk of 'too many people' de-
fines us as our own enemy, summoned to a just
and valiant war against ourselves, in the course of
which (as always in war) personal freedom will
have to count for nothing.

Is that really a 'just war', as regards the cause at
stake and not only the weaponry involved? Are we
really hateful beings, a cancer, a pollution of this
fair planet's surface? Could our self-loathing—
direct, or projected upon some human adversary
whom we equate with Satan—be fully justified?

Conceivably. To read history or the newspapers
is to get a distinct impression that we are a race of
demons, the children of some devil or demiurge,
best prevented.

Yet there are certain controversial viewpoints
from which God might be said to look upon our
existence in some more favourable light.

Our existence: not necessarily our behaviour, or our comfort and health and longevity and afflu- ence.

V

People for God?

What if the background thinking that we brought to this question were neither totalitarian nor Manichaean but Christian? What if human beings existed—primarily, over-ridingly—for God?

Here we reach the heart of the matter. Given the existence and primacy of God as our first beginning and our last end, it is hard to see how 'too many people' can mean anything at all. Those earlier considerations will not vanish altogether. We shall still need 'society', since *Homo sapiens* is a social animal like some dogs, not a solitary animal like some cats; and as we all know, the Christian Gospel intensifies social obligation rather than eliminating it. Beyond that, we shall still need government and even 'the State', though our fallen nature—while making government necessary—means that it can never be trusted. In the same way, we shall still need to recognise the hardship of most human existence and the greater comfort of the reasonably 'high-quality' life. But we shall need to see all such questions as secondary. They concern the conditions of our existence but not its purpose. We cannot define our *raison d'être*, without remainder, in such terms as those: we cannot set statistical and other limits, beyond which our existence ceases to be a good thing.

The matter could be stated in slightly more theological terms. If we make society or the State into our sole *raison d'être*, our first beginning and last end, our God in fact (and we do exactly that when we speak of socially superfluous people) we shall be committing the prime sin of idolatry: if we deny the inherent goodness of our own being, we shall be falling away from Christian theism and flirting (to say the least) with the ancient heresy of the Manichees. A Christian will hope to avoid both evils; and at a different level, he will dislike the intensely vulgar sense now given to such expressions as 'the high-quality life'. How would the saints and martyrs have understood that expression 'standards of living' as well?

Above all (I suggest) he will naturally or instinctively refrain from thinking and speaking in terms of 'too many people'. As considered in a Christian perspective, even in a strongly theistic perspective of any sort, that becomes an almost empty concept in theory and an utterly empty concept in practice. Too many for God's purposes? Faith gives us an inkling of what those purposes are. But when it comes to the question of how many people will best accomplish those purposes, faith and reason are equally silent.

There remains an extremely rarefied sense in which that question has a kind of answer, unknown and unknowable to ourselves. For scientific and religious reasons alike, we know that humanity cannot continue for ever on this planet. There must come a moment—tomorrow, or in the immeasurably distant future—when our human and historical story comes to an end. At that moment, there will be a certain finite number, the sum total of all the human beings who have existed from first to last. God will know that number if he thinks arithmetically, but we have no reason to suppose that any human being will ever know it.

On any Christian understanding of eschatology and purpose, that number—like everything else—will implement the unfathomable will of God. So we shall then be able to say (if so preoccupied and so informed) that God wanted x billion people to exist, and that they therefore did and do.

Will we be able to say that x billion plus one would have been 'too many people' for God's purposes?

But these are rarefied thoughts indeed, useless for any present purpose of judgment or policy. Various writers have considered the question of 'an optimum population' for this earth and have invariably floundered about in great confusion, mostly because of reluctance to ask why it should be considered a good thing for human beings to exist *at all*. But 'an optimum population' for Heaven—that's a subject about which we can only make jokes in doubtful taste. We can say nothing to the purpose about it, and we ought to follow Wittgenstein's sensible advice and keep our silly mouths shut.

Given Christian premises, 'too many people' involves a value judgment which can only be made—if at all—by God. Parents can make it in respect of their potential children, but only because (unlike 'society' or the State) they stand in a God-like or sub-creative relationship towards them; and they need to make it with extreme caution. The only *fully* Christian attitude towards parenthood is: "The Lord may or may not give: the Lord may or may not take away: blessed be the name of the Lord."

Elsewhere, all talk of 'too many people' usurps a divine prerogative.

The case might be better stated in reverse. When people actually do speak of 'over-population', they reveal the extent to which their minds are governed, consciously or not, by non-Christian and even anti-Christian presumptions, broadly totalitarian or broadly Manichaean or both. They say in effect that the goodness or desirability of human existence is not inherent or absolute but highly conditional, almost quantifiable: they see it as a function of certain social and individual variables, its 'value'—in the mathematical sense—being often positive but sometimes zero or negative.

In most cases, the Fallacy of Global Vision and the Myth of Progress will be visibly present and influential as well, each operating in a decidedly anti-Christian sense.

The Fallacy of Global Vision might be described as an over-reaction against Nominalism. We tend some little way towards this fallacy when we speak of 'population' as against 'people', and further when we speak of 'world population'. People actually exist and suffer in the real world, and the only experience we have—good or bad— is that of individuals. 'World population' only exists in statistics and graphs and computers, and we need not worry over any possible sufferings in that quarter.

The Global Vision makes those who take it feel finely objective and responsible: it appeals strongly to officials and politicians. But it always falsifies—in a reductionist or belittling sense—unless kept under the strictest discipline, with constant reference to the concrete and particular. It was given untrammeled indulgence in *Limits to Growth*, a work full of graphs and statistics, powerful in its impact upon the European mind during the 1970s: commenting in some amazement, one writer shrewdly perceived that famous 'model' as a computerised fantasy, concerned not with human beings but "with four billion insects, as seen by the entomologist".[48]

By contrast, the Christian moral emphasis was always particular: you were told to love your neighbour, not humanity or 'Man'—though there are perfectly real senses in which modern communications give us more 'neighbours' than ever before, so widening the scope of that duty. But they are still people, not insects or statistics, and Blake was utterly right in his famous warning about how they need to be treated: "He who would do good to another must do it in Minute Particulars: General Good is the plea of the scoundrel, hypocrite, and flatterer."[49] That great principle has been asserted once again in recent years—by deeds rather than in words—by Mother Teresa of Calcutta.

Global visions of 'General Good' are just about the opposite of what Christians call 'charity', not

[48] *Zero Growth?*, 54.
[49] *Jerusalem*, f. 55, l. 54.

least in this present matter. "No matter how you slice it, population is a numbers game", said Dr. Ehrlich,[50] and he was absolutely right. As played by himself and so many others, it is indeed a game with numbers, while there are actual people who need help.

Beyond that, doomtalk about population appears to be largely motivated by our old friend the Myth of Progress, to which many of us are most inordinately attached, even some Christians; and in this—as in so much else[51]—it resembles doomtalk about Communism and the consequent justification of nuclear weapons. "The threat of overpopulation stands second only to that of nuclear warfare; either can destroy the course of human *progress*",[52] as also could some massive extension of the Russian Empire, and we might be disposed to see all three possibilities as 'disastrous' in more or less the same sense of that word.

But they differ sharply in respect of what they threaten. A big nuclear war would cause a great many of us, perhaps all of us, to die: those weapons, numerous and aimed and ready, consti-

---

[50] *The Population Bomb,* 3-4.

[51] See Appendix.

[52] John B. Calhoun in *Population Control,* edited by Anthony Allison (London: Penguin Books, 1970), 116, emphasis added.

tute a direct threat to human life as such. But when people talk about the menace of Communism or of over-population, they have something different in mind—a threat to the conditions under which human life is lived, and (perhaps above all) a threat to our faith in Progress, our desire to retain a politically and economically optimistic view of the human future. Any major increase in Soviet power would undeniably constitute a set-back to political hopes, to political optimism; and in the same way, population growth is undoubtedly one of the factors that threaten our economic optimism, our belief in a future of ever-increasing affluence for one and all. "All modernized societies conduct their economies on the basis of rising material standards for all citizens":[53] they do indeed, and for many, the consequently optimistic expectations have taken the place of what Christians call 'hope'.

As already suggested, we can never *know* that any conceivable level of world population density would be 'disastrous' in any sense of increasing the sum total of human misery or decreasing the sum total of human happiness: no relevant calculus is possible. But population growth certainly does offer a 'disastrous' threat to the faith in Progress, as currently and precariously cherished by the com-

[53] *Only One Earth,* 177.

fortable. That's at least some part of why comfortable people see it in terms of eschatological doom.

Was that ever a well-founded sort of faith? Was
there ever a real possibility that we might plan and
technologise and arm and contracept ourselves
into a future of universal comfort and plenty? We
may be clever enough for that: I see no reason to
think that we're wise or good enough. As C. S.
Lewis once observed (in *The Abolition of Man*), the
dream of 'Man controlling his own destiny' always comes to nothing or else works out as an
Orwellian nightmare, in dictatorial terms of some
men controlling other men.

'Progress' is a very unreliable and unsuitable
object for what Christians call 'faith'. Not all
things can be realistically seen in the problem-
and-solution terms that we favour so instinctively
in this technological age. We're in God's hands if
there is a God: if there isn't, we're mostly in evil
hands or in no hands at all.

There is a God, and we're for him. That's why
we cannot sit in judgment upon our own existence, our own numbers.

Certain Christians might look with disfavour
upon that statement of the case, as being exces-
sively other-worldly or 'angelic'. Is 'going to
Heaven' the *only* thing that matters? Are we to

shrug off all worldly concerns—all possibilities of disaster, for example—and leave our neighbours' well-being to the providence of God?

The short answer is, of course, that if we have no active concern for our neighbours' well-being, we *shan't* 'go to Heaven'. A Christian's other-worldliness, though necessary, is self-defeating if it promotes or even tolerates any sort of indifference to what happens in this world and this life, to one's neighbour in particular.

Were we to forget this, we might take certain morally outrageous attitudes, seemingly justifiable on the basis that existence is inherently good and that we are for God. "If mere existence is such a tremendous and immeasurable blessing, why can't the poor be content with that?"

We might go further. It certainly is human existence that God appears to value, for its own sake and not for its 'quality' as now understood by the prosperous; and there's a great deal in Scripture and in Catholic theology and spirituality to suggest that he attaches particular value to the unfortunate, the underprivileged, the poor and the sick and the outcast and the hungry and hopeless. It is people of that sort who are his special friends, the ones with whom he identifies on the Cross and in general: they aren't his failures or rejects.

A paradoxical conclusion might seem to follow.

"Well, if poverty and sickness and hunger confer the special friendship of God, won't we be inflicting a spiritual curse upon those whose sufferings we alleviate? Shouldn't we leave them in their more blessed condition?"

Catholic faith includes a number of such apparent paradoxes, caused to seem real by the limitations of our understanding, unreal in fact. We often have to behave *as though* something were the case, while knowing that it is *not* the case. Evangelism is one example. We have to preach the Gospel with the utmost urgency, as though all the unconverted and unbaptised were certain to incur literal damnation, while knowing that God is merciful to all his children. Then there's the old maxim: "Work as though it all depended upon your own efforts; pray as though it all depended upon God alone." A logician might deem it absurd to conduct life on the basis of two contradictory principles or presumptions. But it works, and a good theology of prayer and grace should help us to understand why there's no real contradiction at all.

So with poverty and hunger and the other tribulations of the 'low-quality' life. We have to behave as though the sufferings of other people—though not our own—constituted an absolute and unqualified evil, while knowing that temporal comfort is a dangerous thing and that nobody ever came close to God without suffering.

The paradox is an easy one in fact. We shall be judged, partially at least, on the basis of how we treated Christ in those special friends of his (Mt 25:31-45): we can't give them God's kind of love since we are not God, but we can give them our human kind of love, which must always include a desire to relieve suffering wherever it exists. We may or may not succeed, but we shall need to have been people who tried.

In this context of population and the things said about it, with the Judgment constantly in mind, we should look with disapproval and even with terror upon much of what 'the world' values most highly—'affluence', for example. Will those affluent people be told that they have already received their reward? We should certainly look with disapproval and terror on the world's present allocation of resources, its order of priorities. "It is a damning indictment of human nature that the advanced nations have used funds to orbit Mars, to put men on the moon, and to develop a fearsome collection of destructive weapons, whilst at the same time over one-third of the people of the world are undernourished or malnourished."[54]

[54] *People Populating,* 153.

If we take the Gospel seriously, we cannot see that word "damning" as a rhetorical exaggeration.

There's much statistical and other evidence to suggest that, in general, human beings are far more interested in killing one another than in feeding one another. That's one spectacular symptom of what we call 'Original Sin'.

It's more than likely, I fear, that certain hasty readers of this book will see it as an attempt to dismiss 'the population problem' from serious consideration, as being unreal or unimportant. More dangerously still, it may be pressed into service among "the easy speeches that comfort cruel men", so reinforcing fortunate people in their complacency. That was the great moral failure of Malthus: he assured his readers that since nothing could be done about the condition of the poor, there was no point in trying. A man might therefore eat a big meal in good conscience while others starved around him.

His picture retains a certain realism: he did at least see the folly of all hope that's based upon revolutionary Utopianism. The human condition is still incurably tragic, if not in one way, then in another; and while a Christian should never be 'fatalistic' in any sense of despairing and withdrawing into some Buddhist or Stoic *apatheia*, he must

always practise "abandonment to divine Providence", expecting no earthly paradise, least of all
as offered by the revolutionary Left.

But with an eye to the whole world's scene, we
can no longer speak quite as Malthus did. "Poverty and hunger are things that we can't do anything about": he gave a certain plausibility to that
comforting idea. But in our time, it has become far
more alarmingly true to say "Poverty and hunger
are things that we don't bother about very much:
they come low in our list of priorities."

No Christian can be happy about that state of
affairs. But what can we *do* about it, in practical
terms?

That question, although of very great importance, lies outside my present subject, outside my
competence as well: I offer no advice about (say)
development in the Third World. As guides to
thought and action in such matters, I do however
recommend the great social encyclicals, as also the
works of G. K. Chesterton and E. F. Schu-
macher.

Having said so much, I am still anxious to fore-
stall one possible misinterpretation. I have argued
at some length that if a Christian seeks fidelity to
the Gospel, to the whole tradition of his Church
and his Faith, he will need to regard 'too many
people' as a simply meaningless expression. That

might indeed be taken as implying that 'the population problem' is unreal or unimportant.

But I intend nothing of the sort: I only mean that by Christian standards, it's inaccurately so named. This book might be summed up as an exercise in relabelling.

Labels matter. Life is full of problems, and we may do something like our best to solve them. But in every case, the lines on which we make the attempt will be governed by our notion of what the problem is; and that will be governed in turn (perhaps unconsciously) by the name commonly given to that problem. If it's an inaccurate or misleading name, we shall be in confusion from the start and unable to achieve much: we shall also be falling away from objectivity, possibly in faith and morals.

So a crucial distinction needs to be drawn at every point. 'The population problem' is an ambiguous expression. It is undeniably true that where population increases, certain new problems arise while certain old problems are exacerbated: a Christian may thus speak without hesitation about 'the problems consequent upon rapid population growth', and should regard them as matter for concern and for any help that may be possible. But he then speaks of problems that people *have*. He crosses a fatal Rubicon if he starts to speak of the 'problem' that people *are*, or will be in some foreseeable future. The existence of human beings does not come under our judgment.

I therefore offer one practical recommendation which is capable of being followed by every Christian, privately or (for some) in public speech and writing. Sooner or later, we shall come across some mention of 'the population problem', 'over-population', or 'too many people'. *We should never let such expressions pass unchallenged.*

The nature of our challenge will depend on the speaker. If he claims to be a Christian—or, for that matter, any kind of theist—we should remind him that if people exist for God, the implied value judgments cannot be made by mortals. He may of course make no such claim: he may be an atheist or agnostic, he may take no interest at all in religious questions, or he may see them as having no relevance to this particular subject. In any such case, we should draw his attention to the philosophical and ideological and even religious stance that he is adopting, perhaps in some very unexamined manner: we should point out that he is saying something far more deeply controversial than "We must do something about world poverty." That won't end the debate. But it should *improve* the debate: that is to say, it should enable primary attention to be drawn to that very primary question of what people are *for*.

Catholics need to be particularly careful: they can so easily be caused to seem indifferent to suffering, by reason of what will probably be called 'moralistic prejudice' or 'ecclesiastical bigotry'. So for tactical reasons—though for other and far greater reasons too—they need to make it abundantly clear that they are *not* indifferent to the sufferings of others, the poor especially. That can be difficult, especially where a punctiliously orthodox Catholicism is associated—as it frequently and confusingly is—with some heartless extreme of political and social and economic and military 'Conservatism'.

A Catholic also needs to steer the discussion away from the moral question of contraception. Sooner or later, that question may prove capable of being by-passed more or less completely. We can at least imagine some new method of birth-control—some development of 'natural family planning', perhaps—which is totally effective, even among poor and illiterate people, and which cannot be faulted by even the most severe of moralists or Popes. That would modify the private question of individual behaviour: it would make no difference at all to the value judgments implied in 'too many people'.

The main thing is to get the so-called population problem broken up into its component parts—which are real enough—and to get each of these named accurately and then approached on whatever lines may be appropriate and feasible. There's the 'food problem', for example, which is all too real in many places: it may be broken down into the 'food production problem' and the 'food distribution problem', the latter being perhaps more serious. Within the former, the 'water and irrigation problem' is often crucial, as is the 'soil-fertility problem'. Then we have the 'environmental problem', its chief components being waste, pollution, and over-urbanisation.

That is not meant to be a definitive analysis; and within it, each of those component problems does already receive some practical attention and should receive more.

But if we are Christians, we should never lump them together and speak of the 'population problem', or allow others to do so without challenge. People undoubtedly *have* problems, inevitable or (quite often) self-inflicted, what with our habitual sin and folly: they create problems for one another, they confront you and me and the government with problems that may or may not prove more or less soluble. But if they exist for divine and not only for human purposes, we must never talk as though they could *be* a problem. In whatever quantities they exist at any given moment within the historical process—past, present, or future—

they constitute a fixed and sacred *datum*, humanity or 'Man', better named as 'Adam' or 'Christ': they are then the starting-point from which "the troubles of our proud and angry state" derive their momentary pattern.

Judgments upon human behaviour are always possible and sometimes need to be adverse, even severe. But if anyone passes quantitative or other judgment upon human *existence*—actual or potential, now or in the future—he will be usurping a jurisdiction that belongs to God alone.

That's no usurpation for the totalitarian mind, since all jurisdiction belongs to the State: it's a righteous usurpation for the Manichaean mind, since the creator of mankind is evil. But a Christian needs to think differently.

———

Appendix

At various points in this book, I have hinted at the curious parallelism that exists between two widely supported causes of our time—the cause of population control and the cause of nuclear deterrence. Between the two, I see a close similarity of logical structure and I suspect an affinity in psychology and motivation.

It may therefore be interesting to consider the two a shade more systematically, though briefly, and in parallel. The following similarities spring to mind.

1. In either case, we are warned of a possible disaster which is seen in final, even eschatological terms. I have mentioned the tendency of many writers to speak as though over-population threatened our very 'survival': in just the same way, other writers speak as though any extension of the Russian Empire would constitute a final doom, an end of all things for those affected. It would undoubtedly be a very great evil, a set-back for various kinds of well-being and hope, comparable to the numerous other evils and set-backs that

have punctuated human history. Yet like the demographic fear, this political fear is commonly discussed in the inappropriately strong language of eschatology. So far as human conduct is concerned, that language should be reserved for the very real possibility of an all-out nuclear holocaust, a termination of everybody.

2. In either case, a technological rather than a moral or religious remedy is proposed: contraception and abortion and sterilisation in the one matter, nuclear deterrence in the other.

3. But each lacks credibility, since each calls for a radical, unprecedented, and permanent modification of human behaviour. In the one matter, doom can only be averted if the unbiological practice of having very small families is either chosen or else enforced, universally and for ever: in the other matter, the twin dooms of nuclear war and of Soviet expansionism can only be averted if politicians display a long-term sagacity and restraint that has never characterised their tribe in the recorded past.

4. In either case, the cause is politically slanted, being favoured by Conservatives and the political Right. In the West, this is entirely obvious where nuclear deterrence is concerned; and in this matter as in some others, the Soviet regime must be regarded as 'conservative' in the highest degree. In

1983, I had the amusing experience of corresponding simultaneously with certain Catholic Conservatives and with the Soviet Peace Committee, the subject being nuclear deterrence; and about that, both parties thought and argued on precisely similar lines.

The fact that population control is also a cause of the Right may be less obvious: it is concealed from many Americans, for example, by their country's arbitrary politicisation of the abortion issue. But it's been a fact ever since Malthus was denounced so fiercely by Marx and Proudhon, and it dominated the Bucharest Conference of 1974.

Population control is something that rich and powerful people want to impose upon poor and weak people: it's also (in practice and for the most part) something which white people want to impose upon black and brown people.

I have never been any sort of Leftist or 'Liberal'. But in these two matters alike—as also in certain social and economic matters—any Catholic who tries to think with the Gospel and the Church will incur the distrust of the political Right. I have often incurred it on precisely those lines.

5. In either matter, the protagonists' motivations cry out for cynical comment. The cause of 'birth-control', as it used to be called, has long been advocated for its own sake by certain people,

even in those earlier days when *under*-population could be seen as the great danger: it is hard not to suspect them of welcoming all this doomtalk about population, as offering so splendid a justification for their already sacred cause. In just the same way, while those who favour nuclear deterrence invariably claim to be men of peace, concerned only with the prevention of war, they nearly always display great bellicosity or hawkishness of mind. 'Our country's armed might' is, for most of them, as sacred and emotionally-loaded a concept as 'birth-control' is for those others; and if you suggest that the Soviet threat may be less serious than they suppose, they react not only with disbelief but also with *anger*, like that of an alcoholic from whom you propose to steal the bottle. For them, this world *has to* be such as to make massively genocidal armaments relevant to its problems.

I thus generalise on the basis of very wide experience. It may be relevant to add that in either matter, big commercial interests are involved.

6. And in either matter, the Catholic conscience comes in for much falsification. It is well known that Church teaching, when traditional and orthodox and official, condemns those technologies of population control as being inherently sinful: also, that many theologians and others retain the

Catholic name while partially or totally rejecting that teaching and tradition. Political considerations cause it to be much less widely known that in the other matter as well, there can be—and are—strictly comparable departures from traditional moral theology. One point of departure is the relationship between 'conditional intention' and 'immediate formal guilt': another is the distinction between 'intention' and 'motivation'. Others lie in the area of 'indirect action' and 'double effect'; and more generally, situational and consequential moralities tend to displace our traditional principle that the end does not justify the means.

At a deeper level, the discussion of both matters is coloured by a certain rejection of the Cross, a desire to retain present comforts at any cost in moral fidelity.

I thus detect a sixfold parallelism between those two causes, those two urgencies, and the associated debates.

Their psychological affinity seems to me threefold. Sexual passions are involved, for one thing, obviously in any question that concerns procreation and rather less obviously in any question that concerns violence and killing.

Two further points, closely relevant to both matters, have already been mentioned. There's the Myth of Progress, for one thing. We all like comfort and dislike hardship. But quite apart from that, many of us appear to find it psychologically unendurable to envisage and world's future as continuing in its ancient pattern of ups and downs, of calamitous reverses interspersed with happier times. We *must* have some way of seeing it as a continuous up-and-up! But that's a 'must' of pure psychology, not of history or experience or logic or faith.

Then, there's the sadly arrogant tendency of exceptionally fortunate people to suppose that theirs is the only tolerable sort of existence.

DATE DUE

APR 20 '88			
MAY 4 '88			

DEMCO 38-297